YOUR KNOWLEDGE HAS

- We will publish your bachelor's and master's thesis, essays and papers

- Your own eBook and book - sold worldwide in all relevant shops

- Earn money with each sale

Upload your text at www.GRIN.com
and publish for free

The European Dept Crisis. Why it occured and what we can learn of it

Christian Block

GRIN :)

Bibliographic information published by the German National Library:

The German National Library lists this publication in the National Bibliography; detailed bibliographic data are available on the Internet at http://dnb.dnb.de.

ISBN: 9783346264282
This book is also available as an ebook.

Print and binding: Books on Demand GmbH, Norderstedt, Germany
Printed on acid-free paper from responsible sources.

The present work has been carefully prepared. Nevertheless, authors and publishers do not incur liability for the correctness of information, notes, links and advice as well as any printing errors.

GRIN web shop: https://www.grin.com/document/935854

Bachelor Thesis – Finance Major

The European Sovereign Debt Crisis: drawing future implications from a root cause analysis.

Literature review by Christian Block

Date: January 31th 2020

Inhaltsverzeichnis

List of abbreviations

EMU	Economic and Monetary Union
SGP	Stability and Growth Pact
GDP	Gross Domestic Product
GIPS countries	Greece, Ireland, Portugal, and Spain
Current account	Represents a country's imports and exports balance
ABS	Asset-Backed Securities
EU	European Union
IMF	International Monetary Fund
ESM	European Stability Mechanism
EMF	European Monetary Fund

Chapter 1: Introduction

The Euro celebrated its 20th anniversary last year (2019) and is known worldwide as a symbol of the unity and sovereignty of the European Union. Introduced at a time by people and states who had fought a relentless war against each other in the same century, the Euro is one of the greatest achievements of modern times. Today, a European generation is growing up that no longer knows any national currency and does not understand why it is so important to protect the Euro as a common currency. However, it is precisely this generation that has to deal with the national debt crisis, which has become one of the greatest economic policy challenges that the united Europe has faced since the existence of the monetary union.

The purpose of this thesis is to help understand the development of the European sovereign debt crisis from the introduction of the Euro to the present day. In this context, special attention is paid to the analysis of the causes, since these must be understood fundamentally in order to avoid the repetition of the same process in the future. The key motivation behind this paper is that with current declines in economic growth and inverse yield curves pointing towards a recession, it is more important than ever to understand past developments to avoid such collapses in the future. Past empirical research often overlooks this important forward-looking function; further, most works were published immediately after the financial crisis, with relatively few recent contributions. Clearly, the relevance for society as a whole is given, as implications of economic crises as extremely widespread and caused devastation for many. As globalization has only increased in the decade thereafter, any coming recession would be worse than those experienced before.

This thesis can be divided thematically into three major areas, to ultimately answer the questions of how the European debt crisis came to be, what weaknesses within the EMU led to this, and what lessons can be drawn from it all. First, the developments of the EMU from its inception up to the financial crisis in 2007. Second, the financial crisis and its direct impact on the European sovereign debt crisis. Third, the thesis gives an outlook on the current situation eight years after the outbreak of the crisis and provides suggestions for future research. It should be noted that this thesis deals with the main features of the development of the public debt crisis and that an analysis of any and all factors involved goes beyond the scope of the thesis. During the empirical investigation the focus is on the seven key countries of the Euro area. These include the four largest European economies and the countries most affected by the Euro crisis: France, Germany, Italy and Spain, as well as Portugal, Greece and Ireland.

1.1 Institutional design of the European monetary union

The monetary integration in Europe started with the launch of the Euro, the single currency of the European Union. The Euro was adopted on 1 January 1999 by 11 of the 15 Member States of the Union and was a well-prepared and long-awaited moment in the history of Europe. The introduction of the Euro on the financial markets started on 1 January 1999 and the circulation of notes and coins in 2002.

The Maastricht Treaty of 1991 established the conditions for the monetary union. National governments were required to make serious restructuring of public finance and government spending. Restrictive national monetary policies and an independent central bank were meant to promote European integration. In addition, the Maastricht convergence criteria were established; created to ensure an optimal functioning of the monetary union and for all members to work towards an economically heterogeneous community, the criteria included the stability of long-term interest rates, price levels, exchange rates and public finances (Consolidated version of the treaty of the functioning of the European union, 2012).

Proposed by the German government in 1995, the SGP, designed to ensure that countries also adhere to financial discipline in the EMU after accession, was implemented. The SGP offered a set of fiscal rules intended to prevent countries of the EMU from spending beyond their means. A state's budget deficit was not allowed to exceed 3% of GDP, with national debt at a maximum of 60% of GDP. Failure to abide by these rules are punished with fines up to 0.5% of the GDP (Maria Green Cowles and Michael Smith, 2000).

Chapter 2: Development of the EMU 1999-2007

The following analysis deals with the economic development of the European Monetary Union from its formation in 1999 until the financial crisis of 2007. First, the macroeconomic differences between the northern and southern economies are presented. Second, the reasons for the emergence of current account imbalance between different countries are reviewed. Third, the development of the public and private debt is examined. Last, the emergence and reasons for the housing and banking bubble are discussed.

2.1 Macroeconomic differences

Figure 1. Percentage of GDP composed of Exports for Selected European Economies

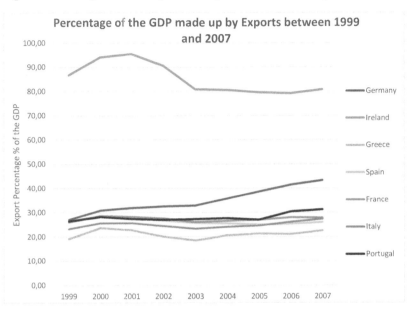

(World Bank 2020, own representation)

Figure 1 shows the percentage of the GDP made up by Exports between 1999 and 2007.

It can be observed that the economies of northern countries such as Germany and Ireland receive a larger share of their GDP from exports, compared to southern European economies such as Portugal, Spain and Italy, which gain only a small percentage of their GDP from exports with all of them below the EMU average. This suggests that the respective countries have different economic approaches with specific national differences. While Germany is pursuing an export-oriented growth model, countries like Spain or Italy following a demand-oriented growth model (Peter A. Hall, 2014).

Export-oriented countries are focused on enhancing international competitiveness, with strategies including wage-setting by collective bargaining, large investments in education and employment, and well-established inter-company relations that are beneficial to research and innovation. These countries pursue strategies based on export-led growth, that is productivity growth of export goods is greater than the proportional wage growth and domestic demand.

Demand-driven countries, however, are less effective at increasing global competitiveness. Trade unions are strong, but they compete for the right to represent workers and are not in a position to coordinate wage levels (Bob Hancke, 2013). Demand growth strategies are based on expansion of domestic demand and their focus is the employment for the service sector and a low skilled workforce. Low-cost labour often provides the competitive advantage for companies in these countries. As demand growth macroeconomic policies are prone to increase inflation rates, an often-used tool by these governments was the periodic devaluation of their exchange rates to lower export prices and make imports more expensive, thereby offsetting the impact of inflation on the trade balance (Peter A. Hall, 2014).

Considering this diversity of economies within EMU, the ECB faced a problem, as it was responsible for a monetary policy that was appropriate and suitable for the entire union.
From 1999-2006, the ECB engaged in a policy of low interest rates designed to stimulate demand, credit growth, and housing markets in the northern economies (European Parliament, 2019). This low-inflation approach favoured the northern economies, which were able to pursue their export-oriented growth strategies and further enhance their exports. Trading partners within the EMU were not able to depreciate their currency anymore which further strengthened the trade position of the export economies. Subsequently, northern export economies started building up current account surpluses.

Southern economies, however, encountered serious challenges. GIPS countries experienced atypically high growth and inflation rates compared with its European partners, resulting in low or even negative real interest rates from 2000. In this environment people are incentivized to spend cash, rather than to save it at the bank and incur a guaranteed loss. Consequently, investment and consumption are boosted, as is aggregate demand, which in turn may lead to even higher inflation rates. Countries with higher-than-average inflation rates experience an increase in price levels that is too rapid, and they therefore suffer a loss in price competitiveness, while countries with relatively low inflation rates gain in price competitiveness. Hence, export demand tends to decline in countries with higher inflation rates and domestic producers lose domestic market share due to less competitive prices (Jakob de Haan, Marco Hoeberichts, Renske Maas and Federica Teppa, 2016).

2.2 Current account imbalances

Whereas in the past inflationary countries would have simply devalued their currency to restore their competitiveness, this was no longer possible in the EMU. As a result, inflation stayed high, the countries' exports became uncompetitive, and domestic demand was rising. In addition, there was a capital flow from export-led countries to countries with strong domestic demand. Countries like Germany started to invest their payment surpluses into the GIPS countries, thus floating the countries with cheap credits and overall reducing the cost of capital.

These new credits exaggerated the expansion in southern economies and with it the inflation. The ECB was now confronted with a choice, as it "could have used its monetary instruments to reduce rates of inflation in southern Europe but doing so would have risked contraction in the north" (Hall 2014, p. 1228). The ECB opted for a policy that ensured monetary stability in the northern countries but increased inflation in the southern countries.

Figure 2. Overview of Current Account Balance as Share of GDP

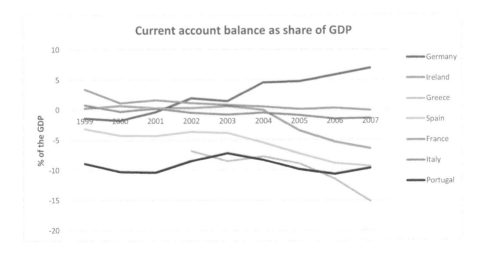

(Eurostat, own representation)

Figure 2 shows the significant differences between Germany, which follows an export-led economy, and the GIPS countries that pursue a domestic demand model. While Germany still had a slight deficit at the introduction of the EMU, its current account balance as a percentage of GDP rose sharply in the following years and reached its highest point in 2007 at almost 7% of GDP. On the other hand, countries such as Spain, Greece or Ireland, recorded a steady current account deficit ever since joining the EMU.

Yet, differences in the current account balance do not always have to be seen as a bad sign. Capital flows from abroad can be used to boost the economy and finance long-term investments. For the most part, however, these loans in the GIPS countries were not used for investments, where the income from such investments could later be used to pay interest and repay principal, but for private consumption and the purchase of real estate (Renate Neubäumer, 2011). The consequence was an accumulation of debt in the GIPS countries.

2.3 Private and public debt development 1999-2007

While the high debt levels of the countries prior to the monetary union would have caused high yields on government bonds, the introduction of a monetary union led to a strong convergence of interest rates.

Figure 3. Overview of Interest Rates on 10-year state bonds in the EMU

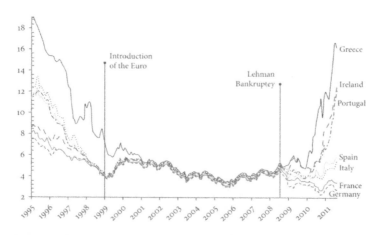

FIGURE   1   *Interest rates on 10-year government bonds (%)*

(Bill Lucarelli, 2013)

Figure 3 illustrates the convergence of the interest rates that has taken place within the monetary union. It can be seen that before 1999, and thus before the EMU, interest rates differed widely. However, this changed, and a strong convergence can be seen from the year 2000 onwards. Former high-interest countries such as Spain, Portugal or Italy, as well as Greece, benefited from the integration of the capital markets and enjoyed similarly low interest rates as had previously the Deutschemark. This suggests that investors ignored the country-specific risks and regarded the countries in the EMU as equal in risk.

In the years leading up to the financial crisis, Europe and the USA initiated a phase of loose budget restrictions on a larger scale, from which the private sector, in addition to the governments, increasingly benefited. These capital flows provided GIPS countries such as Ireland and Spain with growth rates far above the Euro area average. Nevertheless, it was not the public sector that kept its level of debt or even reduced it, but rather the private sector that accumulated large amounts of debt prior to the financial crisis of 2007.

Figure 4. Gross State Debt as a Share of GDP in Selected European Countries

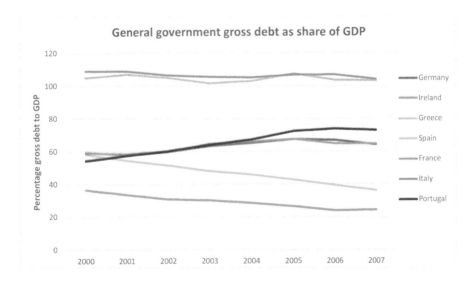

(Eurostat, own representation)

Figure 4 illustrates the amount of public debt in relation to the GDP from 1999 until 2007.

It can be seen that only two of the seven countries are well above the debt ceiling of 60%. All other debt ratios are below or very slightly above it. On closer inspection, the countries can be divided into three groups. The first group consists of Greece and Italy, both of which had a debt ratio of well over 90% when they adopted the Euro. The debt limit set by the Maastricht Treaty and the Stability and Growth Pact was never complied with by either country at any time. However, Italy reduced its debt by as much as 10%. Although Spain's debt ratio of 61% was slightly above the agreed level, the government managed to reduce it to 36% by 2007. Ireland's debt was 46.6% at the beginning and even fell to below 24%. These two countries followed the Stability and Growth Pact agreement, setting the best example by far. Both Germany and France complied with the targets only between 2000 and 2003. In the following years the 60% limit was not complied with anymore. Even Portugal met the criteria at the beginning, but the debt rose sharply in the following years. The Euro zone as a whole reduced its debt from 72% (1999) to 66% (2007) (Eurostat).

Figure 5. Private Debt as a Share of GDP in Selected European Countries

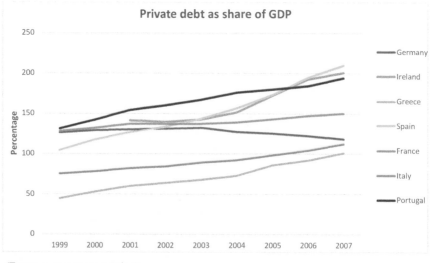

(Eurostat, own representation)

10

While deficits in the public sector have remained stable or in some cases have been reduced significantly since 1999, external indebtedness has occurred primarily in the private sector.

Excessive credit lending to households and corporations skyrocketed between 2002 and 2007; lending to businesses and households increased from almost $1000 billion to almost $2500 billion in the US and from 50 billion to more than 200 billion in the Euro area. The GIPS countries in particular accumulated a high level of external debt. Spain, Greece, and Portugal alone held almost 1200 billion Euros of debt in 2007 (Renate Neubäumer, 2011). Most of the credit flows primarily came from northern European countries, China, and the USA, who invested their export surpluses into the growing southern economies. Figure 5 shows that all countries recorded a strong increase in private debt before 2007, most of them well over 100% of GDP.

Chapter 3: Real estate bubble

One reason for the sharp increase in private debt in many countries was the emergence of a real estate bubble. Facilitated by excessive bank lending, various factors contributed to the rise in house prices and completions of new properties at the beginning of the twenty-first century. The economic upturn of recent years caused immigration into the European Union. Especially countries like Spain, whose GDP grew by about 30% between 2000 and 2007, experienced a particularly high immigration from Eastern European and Latin American countries. Demographic shifts, however, are not the sole reason for the increased demand for properties. Low interest rates and stock market volatility, especially after the dotcom crisis of 2000-2001, tempted many investors to invest their money into real estate (Gala Cano Fuentes, Aitziber Etxezarreta Etxarri, Kees Dol and Joris Hoekstra, 2013).

European banks granted more and more cheap loans to the public, thereby increasing private debt and enabling the real estate sector to flourish. Investment in residential construction almost tripled in Greece between EU accession and 2007. The share of GDP rose from 6% (1999) to 12.5% in 2007. The Irish economy also benefited strongly from the property boom. GDP rose by 56% between 1999 and 2007, which was in fact even stronger than in Greece and Spain (Renate Neubäumer, 2015). During this period, numerous jobs were created in the GIPS economies, in particular in the construction industry. Prices and wages rose steadily, resulting in even higher inflation. The average inflation rate in the GIPS countries was around 3% between 1999 and 2007, resulting in a higher price increase of 11% to 15% compared to Germany in 2007 (Renate Neubäumer, 2011).

The result of this was that current account deficits of the southern European GIPS countries rose sharply until 2007, to 10% of GDP in Spain and Portugal and 14.5% of GDP in Greece. In contrast, Germany achieved a current account surplus of 7.5% of GDP, after its current account had been slightly in deficit at the beginning of monetary union (Renate Neubäumer, 2011).

Chapter 4: Banking bubble and the resulting financial crisis

A decisive factor contributing to the emergence of the crisis was the European banking system and its excessive credit policy prior to 2008.

European banks and foreign investors took advantage of the rising domestic demand in the GIPS countries and granted loans to the population on a broad basis. The continuing boom of the real estate sector in many countries at the beginning of the 2000s tempted many banks to issue loans for commercial property, often without questioning the solvency of the creditors. As a result, Mortgage Backed securities became increasingly popular. Because single mortgage loans proved to be a poor investment opportunity, securitisation was used to bundle a large number of individual mortgages into so-called ABS (asset-backed securities). This process made it possible to transform a local mortgage into a globally tradable security in which hedge funds and banks could easily invest. The highly complex construction of real estate financing meant that even the largest rating agencies did not recognise the high risk of the securities and rated them far too positively. As a result, the international market became floated with over graded subprime mortgages (Kagan, J.,2020).

Similar developments were observed in other European countries and the USA. Major banks were highly leveraged and exposed to the asset backed security market, and accordingly subject to a cascade of default risk. The insolvency of the US investment bank Lehman Brothers on 15 September 2008 marked the start of the biggest economic crisis of the 21st century. Triggered by revaluations on the stock market by the rating agencies in the previous year, the US real estate bubble burst and pulled the global economy into a recession.

The trade in real estate securities dropped by 97% from $1.9 trillion in 2006 to about $53 billion in 2009. The crisis quickly spread around the world, as many European banks were heavily indebted with securities from the US. The consequences were write-offs worth billions and the collapse of the European banking and real estate sector. The GIPS countries, which in the years preceding the financial crisis benefited in particular from the upturn in the real estate sector, were facing considerable economic losses. In Greece alone, there was a shortfall of around 20 billion euros of money that had previously been invested in construction. In Spain, there was a loss of 1.8 million jobs in construction industry.

Hit by this economic downturn, the situation worsened further as most of the GIPS countries were still in need of consolidation. Governments had based their GDP and previous spending on the "inflated" real estate bubble and additional credit-financed consumption. With the collapse of the markets, revenues therefore looked much worse and were no longer in line with the new situation.

Finally, the rescue of the banking system by the respective governments was the final blow that dragged Europe into the sovereign debt crisis, triggered by the excessive indebtedness of private households, especially those with mortgages and consumer credit and the resulting credit defaults. Greece alone had to spend around 20% of its GDP on the recapitalisation of domestic banks. In Ireland, which was hit hardest by the banking crisis, this figure was as high as 35% of GDP (Renate Neubäumer, 2015). While the primary feature in 2008 and for most of 2009 was the stability of the banking system, the markets for government debt remained relatively calm (Philip R. Lane, 2012).

This, however, changed during the course of 2009 as the extent of the recession and rising estimates of potential losses of the banking sector on subprime loans increased. The lack of consolidation in recent years was particularly noticeable in the GIPS countries and further exacerbated the financial situation. For example, Greece's creditworthiness was downgraded from A- to BBB+ at the end of 2009, setting off a chain reaction through a major loss in investor confidence that spread throughout Europe, increasing interest rates across the union and forcing the EU to enforce an initial aid package to avoid the bankruptcy of multiple countries. The EU rescue fund of 750 billion euros was approved by the European Union in May 2009 and was largely accepted by the struggling GIPS countries (Bernd Riegert, 2012).

Figure 6. Government Gross Debt in Relation to GDP

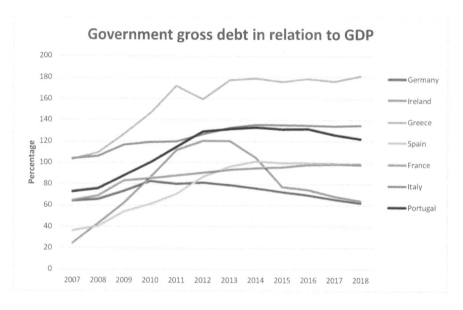

(Eurostat, own representation)

As shown above, the debt ratio increased sharply in almost all countries with the outbreak of the financial crisis. Greece's already high level of debt rose exorbitantly, as well as Italy's and Portugal's. Their debt reached in 2018 181%, 135% and 122% respectively. However, the most serious developments took place in Spain and Ireland. Before 2007, these were the only countries with a debt level of less than 60%. Between 2008 and 2013 Spain more than doubled from 40% to 99% and Ireland almost tripled from 42% to 120% their debt. By 2018 Ireland and Germany achieve a debt reduction to almost 60% and thus almost complying with the Maastricht convergence rules (Eurostat).

Figure 7. Private Sector Debt, Non-Consolidated in Relation to GDP

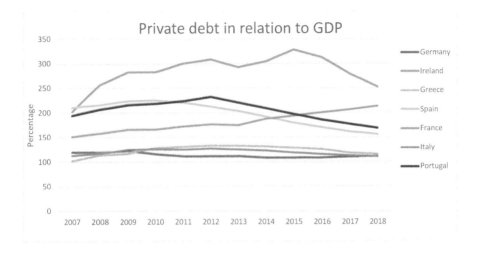

(Eurostat, own representation)

After 2008, the development of private debt was contrary to that of the public sector. The rapid increase in the years before 2007 ended with the financial crisis. Germany, Greece, and Italy shared a similar debt development of the years and reached a debt level of about 110% in 2018. Spain and Portugal were able to reduce their debt from 2010 and 2012 onwards, achieving in 2018 155% and 167% respectively. Ireland could only achieve a sustainable debt reduction from 2015 onwards, reaching 250% in 2018. France is the only example of consistently undiminished growth in debt.

Chapter 6: Conclusion of the Root Cause Analysis

The structural framework of the monetary union was criticised from its inception. In essence, the central problem was that the ECB was responsible for monetary policy at the European level, while budget and fiscal policy remained at the national level. This lack of a central fiscal policy as well as the convergence of interest rates proved to be a weakness of the union, as individual countries had a greater incentive to accumulate debt.

Early policies, like the Stability and Growth Pact, were adopted to identify and prevent misalignments in national budgetary policies. Penalties, however, were not or only very rarely enforced. In addition, the convergence criteria and SGP were only limited to public debt. As there was no surveillance instrument for the private or banking sector at that time, debt developments remained undiscovered for a long period of time. Instruments such as the no-bailout clause was a complete contrast to the solidarity declarations of the European Union which thus became virtually meaningless. Also, mechanisms such as the lender-off-last-resort or the possibility of devaluing one's own currency were not available to the individual countries, thus depriving them of the opportunity to react adequately to the financial crisis. All in all, membership in the monetary union was in itself a considerable disadvantage for a state in the Euro zone.

In addition, different current account balances and unilateral capital flows also destabilised the Union. GIPS countries recorded a steadily growing current account deficit while countries such as Germany recorded a growing current account surplus. Capital flows, however, were mainly used by private people for consumption and housing construction, but not for investments where the income could be used to pay interest. A growing construction bubble was the consequence. Thus, macroeconomic imbalances and institutional weaknesses in the architecture of monetary union contributed to the vulnerability of some Euro area countries.

The financial crisis exposed the economic differences between the individual countries and increased risk premiums of government bonds. Capital outflows affected GIPS countries that were dependent on capital from abroad. Economic downturn led to a decline in demand, decreased government revenue and an increase in public debt. With the disclosure of Greece's unsound budgetary policies, investors finally began to question the sustainability of the public debt of some Euro area countries. This resulted in significant price losses for government bonds, which was particularly problematic for financial institutions. Since banks hold particularly high shares of government bonds of a country in which they are domiciled, the fall in price had an indirect effect on the credit institutions. The additional bursting of the real estate bubble and the resulting defaulting loans pushed the European banking system to the brink of collapse. In order to prevent the latter, banks had to be recapitalised by the state, which in turn threatened the solvency of the states. This led to a downward spiral in which the banks' credit ratings deteriorated further due to the concentration of domestic government bonds on the banks' balance sheets. It can thus be concluded that the European sovereign debt crisis was not only due to the misconduct of some European countries, but that the financial crisis has led to a transfer of private debt to public debt.

In summary, it can be stated today that the markets have not yet fully recovered from the crises and countries such as Italy and Greece have not shown any sustainable reduction in debt. Moreover, the low interest rate policy of the central banks tempts many investors and countries to spend excessively again, but not to save or reduce their debts. Even at the World Economic Forum of Davos 2020, IMF head Kristalina Georgieva warns against new speculative bubbles and debt excesses triggered by the low interest rate policies of central banks (Holger Zschäpitz, 2020).

A second financial crisis at this stage would be impossible to manage for the EMU and would most likely lead to the collapse of the union. This is why many want Europe to be better prepared for a new financial crisis. One idea was put forward by EU Economic and Monetary Affairs Commissioner Pierre Moscovici who presented his reforms at the end of 2017. Amongst other things, the Euro rescue umbrella ESM should be transformed into a European Monetary Fund. The IMF, the International Monetary Fund in Washington, would then no longer be the decisive rescue authority for distressed EU countries, but instead a European Monetary Fund. The EMF would be responsible to rescue crisis states such as Greece with aid packages in an emergency or rescue distressed banks such as in Italy (Ralph Sina, 2017).

6.1 Future Research

Given the impossibility of the global economy to handle an economic crisis going forward, it is imperative for future research to analyse which policies best prevent the described developments within the EMU leading up to a financial crisis and general economic instability. The first critical question is whether the level of moral hazard, when an entity takes on more debt knowing that another bears the risk for it, can and should be eliminated or reduced. The debt crisis of 2007 displayed that states were ready to cover for respective financial institutions to avoid even greater negative consequences from the described downward spiral; ultimately financial institutions were not liable for their own mistakes in judgment. Future empirical studies must determine how measures such as penalties, in specific scope and size, can keep struggling economies on track within the EMU. Further, as identified, the convergence criteria and SGP must be extended to the private sector, as the lack of regulations in this area was a key contributor to the past crisis.

Additionally, care must be taken in regard to surveillance instruments and macroeconomic modelling. It is crucial to further optimize forecasting and surveillance models, to maximize the accuracy and reliability of the results these provide. This way, early signs of mismanagement and financial distress can be caught and ideally these developments can be interrupted. Lastly, this analysis

This analysis concludes with a question that is ever more prominent following events like the debt crisis and the more recent Brexit: how sensible is a monetary union in Europe today? The structural flaws of the EMU have been described in detail, as well as the general inappropriateness of a converged monetary and fiscal policy for nations with entirely different economic needs. While an area of research has largely focused on synthesizing recommendations for an improved convergence, there is a literature gap in that there is no comprehensive analysis attempting to answer the question stated above. With ever-changing conditions not only in the EMU but worldwide, it is critical to see whether a growing monetary union is viable in the long-term, and whether or not future crises can truly be avoided at all.

Works Cited

BLOT, C., CREEL, J., & HUBERT, P. (2019). Thoughts on a Review of the ECB's Monetary

Policy Strategy. *Monetary Dialogue Papers*. Retrieved from

https://www.europarl.europa.eu/cmsdata/189493/OFCE-original.pdf

Cowles, M. G. (2001). The State Of The European Union: Risks, Reform, Resistance, and

Revival Volume 5 (1. Aufl.). U.S.A.: Oxford University Press, .

CONSOLIDATED VERSION OF THE TREATY ON THE FUNCTIONING OF THE

EUROPEAN UNION. (2012, October 26). Retrieved January 15, 2020, from https://eur-

lex.europa.eu/legal-content/EN/TXT/PDF/?uri=CELEX:12012E/TXT&from=EN

Deutsche Welle. (n.d.). Fünf Länder unterm Rettungsschirm: DW: 25.06.2012. Retrieved from

https://www.dw.com/de/fünf-länder-unterm-rettungsschirm/a-16048178

European Central Bank. (n.d.). Official interest rates. Retrieved from

https://www.ecb.europa.eu/stats/policy_and_exchange_rates/key_ecb_interest_rates/html/inde

x.en.html

Figure 1: World Bank. (2020). Exports of goods and services (% of GDP) - Germany, Italy,

Spain, Portugal, European Union, France, Ireland, Greece | Data. Retrieved 31 January 2020, from https://data.worldbank.org/indicator/NE.EXP.GNFS.ZS?end=2007&locations=DE-IT-ES-PT-EU-FR-IE-GR&name_desc=false&start=1999&view=chart

Figure 2: Eurostat. (n.d.). Retrieved from https://ec.europa.eu/eurostat/databrowser/view/tipsbp20/default/line?lang=en

Figure 3: Lucarelli, B. (2013). *Endgame for the Euro A Critical History*. London: Palgrave Macmillan UK.

Figure 4: Eurostat. (n.d.). Retrieved from https://ec.europa.eu/eurostat/databrowser/view/sdg_17_40/default/line?lang=en

Figure 5: Eurostat. (n.d.). Retrieved from https://ec.europa.eu/eurostat/databrowser/view/tipspd10/default/line?lang=en

Figure 6: Eurostat. (n.d.). Retrieved from https://ec.europa.eu/eurostat/databrowser/view/sdg_17_40/default/line?lang=en

Figure 7: Eurostat. (n.d.). Retrieved from https://ec.europa.eu/eurostat/databrowser/view/tipspd10/default/line?lang=en

Fuentes, G. C., Etxarri, A. E., Dol, K., & Hoekstra, J. (2013). From Housing Bubble to Repossessions: Spain Compared to Other West European Countries. *Housing Studies, 28*(8), 1197–1217. doi: 10.1080/02673037.2013.818622

Haan, J. de, Hoeberichts, M., Maas, R., & Teppa, F. (2016). Inflation in the euro area and why it matters. *DNB Occasional Studies*. Retrieved from https://www.dnb.nl/en/binaries/1605458_OS14-3_ENG_v9_tcm47-346543.pdf

Hall, P. A. (2014). Varieties of Capitalism and the Euro Crisis. *West European Politics, 37*(6), 1223–1243. doi: 10.1080/01402382.2014.929352

Hancké, B. (2013). The missing link. Labour unions, central banks and monetary integration in Europe1. *Transfer: European Review of Labour and Research, 19*(1), 89–101. doi: 10.1177/1024258912469347

Kagan, J. (2020, January 29). Understanding Mortgage-Backed Securities (MBS). Retrieved from https://www.investopedia.com/terms/m/mbs.asp

Lane, P. R. (2012). The European Sovereign Debt Crisis. *Journal of Economic Perspectives, 26*(3), 49–68.

Neubäumer, R. (2011). Eurokrise: Keine Staatsschuldenkrise, sondern Folge der Finanzkrise. *Wirtschaftsdienst, 91*(12), 827–833. doi: 10.1007/s10273-011-1308-5

Neubäumer, R. (2015). Eurokrise: Sparpolitik zweitrangig für den Einbruch der Wirtschaftsleistung in Griechenland? . *Ifo Schnelldiens, 68*(18). Retrieved from https://www.cesifo-group.de/DocDL/sd-2015-18-neubaeumer-eurokrise.pdf

Osullivan, K., & Kennedy, T. (2010). What caused the Irish banking crisis? *Journal of Financial Regulation and Compliance, 18*(3), 224–242. doi: 10.1108/13581981011060808

Tagesschau.de. (2018, June 6). Ein europäischer Währungsfonds bis 2019. Retrieved January 29, 2020, from https://www.tagesschau.de/wirtschaft/eu-reformpaket-103.html

Your key to European statistics. (n.d.). Retrieved from https://ec.europa.eu/eurostat

Zschäpitz, H. (2020, January 29). Verschuldung: IWF fordert Risikopuffer wegen lockerer

Notenbankpolitik - WELT. Retrieved January 30, 2020, from

https://www.welt.de/finanzen/article205420707/Verschuldung-IWF-fordert-Risikopuffer-

wegen-lockerer-Notenbankpolitik.html

YOUR KNOWLEDGE HAS VALUE

- We will publish your bachelor's and master's thesis, essays and papers

- Your own eBook and book - sold worldwide in all relevant shops

- Earn money with each sale

Upload your text at www.GRIN.com and publish for free